Decodable
READER

UNIT 2

SAVVAS
LEARNING COMPANY

ISBN-13: 978-0-32-898864-8
ISBN-10:   0-32-898864-2

8 22

Table of Contents

The Sleds

Written by Alphie Heart

Short e

Fred	Meg	Peg	sled
get	Ned	red	

Consonant _qu_ /kw/

Quin

Initial Consonant Blends

Fred	sled	sleds

High-Frequency Words

a	little	the

1

Peg can get a sled.

Peg can get a little sled.

Meg can get a sled.

Meg can get a big sled.

Quin can get a sled.

Quin can get a red sled.

Get on the sleds!
Get Ned.
Get Fred.

Fix It!

Written by Todd Jacob

Consonant *x*

fix	Max	mix

Closed Syllable CVC

can	fix	Jim	Max
Dad	Jan	Kim	mix

Short *i*

fix	Kim
it	mix
Jim	

High-Frequency Words

do	we

9

Can Jim fix it?
Jim can fix it.

Can Kim fix it?
Kim can fix it.

11

Can Max fix it?
Max can fix it.

Can Jan fix it?
Jan can fix it.

Can Dad do it?
Can Dad fix it?

14

Fix it, Dad!
Dad can fix it.

Dad can mix it.
Dad can fix it.
We can fix it.

16

The Pack

Written by Laura Kennedy

Consonant Pattern -*ck*

back	sack
Jack	Zack
pack	

Consonant *z*

Zack

High-Frequency Words

a

for

17

Jack can pack.
Jack can pack a back sack.

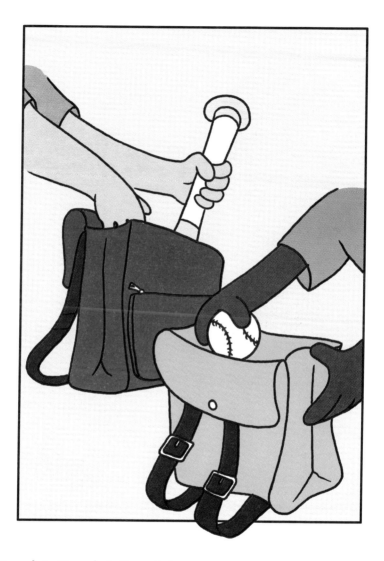

Pack! Pack! Pack!
Pack a sack.

Pack! Pack! Pack!
Pack a sack for Jack.

Zack can pack.
Zack can pack a sack.

Pack! Pack! Pack!
Pack a sack.

Pack! Pack! Pack!
Pack a sack for Zack.

Jack ran.
Zack ran.

Pigs, Wigs, Cats, and Bats

Written by June Adams

Plural -s			Consonant s /z/	
bats	hats	pots	fans	pigs
cats	mats	wigs	has	wigs
fans	pigs			

High-Frequency Words

have	the	two
one	three	we

One fox can nap.
Fox is in the box.

Two pigs sit.
Fat pigs pin on wigs.

Three cats tap.
Tan cats tap on mats.

28

The bats hit.
The bats hit pots.

Cats can tap.
Bats can hit.

Pigs have hats.
Fox has fans.

Tap! Tap! Tap!
We can nap.

A Blue Box

Written by José Soto

Final Consonant Blends	
best	lift
camp	pond
jump	tent
just	

High-Frequency Words				
blue	for	that	use	we
by	from	think	walk	what
do	look	this		

33

Roz, Jim, and I go for a walk.

We can see the camp from here.
The blue pond is by the tent.

We jump on the log.
What is that?
We think we see a blue box!

The log is in the mud.
We can use this to lift up the log.

We try to sit by the log.
We do the best we can.

We look at the box.
It is not what we think.

This is just a blue can!

Big Jobs

Written by Carole Jensen

Inflected Ending -s		**Consonant Pattern -ck**		
digs	naps	Jack	picks	rocks
fills	packs	Nick	Rick	sacks
licks	picks	packs		
mops	rocks			

Consonant s /z/

digs   fills

Word Family -ick

Nick   picks   Rick

High-Frequency Words

a	have	we
do	the	you

Rick digs.
Rick has a hot job.

Lin fills the pan.
The dog licks.
It is a big job.

Nick rocks Quin.
Quin naps.
Nick has a big job.

Kim picks the pods.
It is a big job.

Jack packs the sacks.
Jack did a big job.

Nan mops.
Nan did a top job.

We did big jobs.
Do you have big jobs?

The Moth

Written by Sun Men Chan

Consonant Digraphs *sh*, *th*

Beth	moth	thin
cloth	shin	this
Dash	that	

High-Frequency Words

all	makes	too
goes	they	use
her		

Beth and her dad walk.
They walk with her dog, Dash.

They see a blue moth go by.

Dad steps on a thin stick.

He cut his shin a bit.
That cut it is not too bad.

Beth looks at it for a bit.
Beth goes to her pack.

Dad makes a fix with the cloth.
Dad can use this cloth too.

All is on the mend.

Packing Bags

Written by William Spree

Inflected Ending *-ing*
backing   packing   picking

Inflected Ending *-s*
helps   packs   sits

High-Frequency Words

we

Mom is packing bags.
Dad is packing bags.
Pam helps.

Dad is backing up.
We can get in.

Dad is picking up Jan.
Jan can get in.

Jan and Pam ran.
Mom sits.
Dad sits.

Jan sits.
Pam sits.

Mom packs.
Dad packs.

Mom and Dad sit.
Jan and Pam sit.

Kate Wins the Game

Written by Moira McGinty

Long *a*: *a_e*

brave	game	lake	save	take
Dale	Jane	late	shade	waves
Flames	Kate	makes	shakes	

Consonant Digraph *sh* /sh/

shade   smash

High-Frequency Words

a	her	to
do	the	you

65

Kate can kick the ball.

Mom and Dad take Kate
to her game.
Kate waves to them.

Dale kicks the ball to the shade.
Jane kicks it in the lake.

Dad calls, "You can do it, Kate!"
Mom yells, "Run, Kate, run!"

Kate makes a late kick.
The ball is in the net!

Kate and her smash kick save
the game.
The Flames win!

Mom calls Kate brave.
Dad shakes her hand.

Six Bugs

Written by Rachna Chabra

Long *a: a_e*			
cake	Jane	plane	snake
capes	name	shave	wave
grapes	pale		

Vowel Sound in *ball: a, al, aw*

all	raw
draw	wash
fall	

High-Frequency Words

blue	here	they
five	one	three
for	part	two
four	ride	your

Here is one pale blue bug.
Her name is Jane.

Two pale blue bugs ride in a plane.

Three pale blue bugs go for a shave.

Four pale blue bugs ride on a wave.

Five pale blue bugs all fall in a cake.
Wash your hands here, blue bugs!

Six pale blue bugs all sit on a snake.
Then they draw big bugs in capes.

Six blue bugs stop and sit.
They have part of two raw grapes.

A Fine Pet

Written by Anthony Piero

Long *i*: *i_e*

fine	likes
hide	mine

High-Frequency Words

after	into	many	think	what
don't	know	one	three	you
how	look	see		

Do you know what is in the box?

Don't you see it?

It is mine.
You see many lines on it.

I know how to look after it.
I like to spend time with it.

I make the box safe for it.
It likes to hide.

We cut a snack into three bits.
I set one bit into the box.

Don't you think this is a fine pet?
I know it is a fine pet for me.

88

Where Is Dave?

Written by John Parquette

Consonant c /s/	**Long a: a_e**			
face	cage	face	place	take
lace	Dave	lace	race	
place	**Vowel Sound in ball: a, al**			
race	ball	walk		
Consonant g /j/	**Initial Consonant Blends**			
cage	black	place	steps	

High-Frequency Words

a	here	the
go	my	where

89

Dave is not in his cage.
Where is Dave?

Is Dave on the steps?
Did Dave race up the walk?

Did Dave take my black ball?
Where is it?

Is Dave in bed?
Did Dave get this sock?

This had a lace.
Where did it go?

Is Dave in this place?
Is that his face?

Dave jumps up.
Yes, Dave is here!